D1468663

A California Bestiary

A California
BESTIARY

Rebecca Solnit and Mona Caron

Heyday Books, Berkeley, California

This project was made possible by a generous grant from The Creative Work Fund, a program of the Walter and Elise Haas Fund supported by The William and Flora Hewlett Foundation and The James Irvine Foundation.

Library of Congress Cataloging-in-Publication Data

Solnit, Rebecca.
  A California bestiary / Rebecca Solnit and Mona Caron.
    p. cm.
  Includes bibliographical references and index.
  ISBN 978-1-59714-125-3 (hardcover : alk. paper)
  1. Animals--California. 2. Animals--California--Pictorial works. I. Caron, Mona. II. Title.
  QL164.S65 2010
  591.9794--dc22
                        2009023671

Cover Art: Mona Caron
Book Design: Lorraine Rath
Orders, inquiries, and correspondence should be addressed to:
        Heyday Books
        P. O. Box 9145, Berkeley, CA 94709
        (510) 549-3564, Fax (510) 549-1889
        www.heydaybooks.com

Printed in China by Imago

10 9 8 7 6 5 4 3 2 1

Contents

Acorn Woodpecker
(Melanerpes formicivorus)

The California most often spoken of is Hollywood and Silicon Valley, traffic and crime, sprawl and politics, the California so often announced as having thirty-something million residents. There is another California with tens or hundreds of millions more inhabitants, billions if you count the insects, a state of herbivores and carnivores, of creatures that weigh a thousand pounds and those that could land on the tip of your fingernail, of swimmers, flyers, tunnelers, of creatures as solitary as the wolverine and as communal as ants. California is vast in ways often overlooked. It has more than two hundred species of mammal alone, more than six hundred kinds of birds, and then there are the reptiles, the insects, the arachnids—including new species of spider found in a cave in King's Canyon National Park earlier this decade, along with previously unknown species of millipede, scorpion, and pseudo-scorpion. California's diversity of landscapes, from desert to rainforest, tundra to seashore, creates habitat for its incredible diversity of species. It begat as well the cultural and linguistic diversity of the first human inhabitants and supports an unparalleled variety of contemporary cultures.

Some of the nonhuman immigrants are annual migrants, flying from the far north or the tropics over invisible, irrelevant borders; some inhabit a small portion of California exclusively—the endangered San Francisco garter snake, for example, which exists only on the Peninsula stretching from San Bruno Mountain south, or the Mount Lyell shrew, found only in Yosemite; some inhabit an expanse that goes far beyond the state or some particular ecological niche within it. Acorn woodpeckers live where oak trees flourish in a long western belt stretching from southern Washington to Central America. Or the species does; the individual birds don't go much of anywhere, but defend a territory of oaks from which they harvest the acorns that keep them busy.

These small black-backed woodpeckers with their red yarmulkes are extraordinary for what they do with the acorns: gather them, which squirrels and other animals also do, but then place them, one at a time, narrow end first, in holes they've drilled in tree bark, telephone poles, fence posts, and most recently, amid much ruckus, the sides of buildings in an affluent retirement community in the East Bay. The result is a mosaic wall of up to tens of thousands of acorns, each tapped into a precisely drilled hole, and a supply of food that gives them security throughout the harsher times of year. Maybe it's this prudent storage that gives them the liberty for the rest of their lives, which are antic and apparently much enjoyed. They are noisy, festive, convivial birds who live in extended clans and raise their young in collectives of up to three females and seven males. Multiple females will lay eggs in the same nest, and older siblings will sometimes stay on to raise the young. Early birdwatchers were astounded by these nonnuclear family structures and amused by the birds' acrobatics. The descriptions sometimes sound as though the birds were characters in a comic novel: communards with complicated family dynamics and much clowning, but thrift and a good work ethic, the bird as quintessential California personality.

Bluebelly Lizard, or Western Fence Lizard

(*Sceloporus occidentalis*)

The bestiaries, or books of beasts, of almost a thousand years ago contained much we no longer believe. There is no stone in the heads of toads that neutralizes poison and there are no unicorns at all, so the ability of their horns to likewise undo poison is not particularly helpful either. Those old books were compendiums of known and imagined animals, of eagles and dragons and elephants, with lore about their powers, lives, and meanings, often moral and religious meanings. They were also compendiums of sheer wonder, but the sense of wonder that emerges from scientific knowledge is at least as great, whether it's about the Belding's ground squirrel of the Sierra Nevada that hibernates about eight months a year or the elephant seal that not only can hold its breath underwater for an hour but often does so for twenty minutes or more at a time while sleeping on the shore. Or the blue whale, whose heart is bigger than an American bison and beats about six times a minute, a tenth the speed of ours, or the hummingbird in flight, whose tiny heart beats a thousand times a minute.

Toads can't counteract poison, but bluebelly lizards, it is now known, have a mysterious property in their blood that eliminates Lyme disease from the infected ticks, in their nymph stages, that bite them. They may be why the West Coast is so much less infested with this pernicious disease than the East. The bluebelly's blood now is as marvelous as the toadstone then. But it's important to celebrate the bluebelly for its own sake, for its twenty long toes as delicate as eyelashes, for its ball-bearing eyes, for its grainy camouflaging stripes in tones of dust and shadow, for the secret blue bands of its white underside—two long vertical lines and more blue on its chin, ranging from a soft sky blue in the young and female lizards to a fierce azure that saturates the males in rut.

The official English name of this creature is the western fence lizard, but they were all over the West millennia before fences were, and the California kids I knew called them bluebellies. Bluebellies were everywhere in the California hills when I was growing up, darting away from us, sometimes—like many other lizard species—shedding their tails when one of my brothers tried to catch them, so that the tail stayed behind flapping frantically, a tactic thought to have evolved to distract predators. I have seen thousands of bluebellies, held dozens, perhaps hundreds, but only twice have I seen the intensely blue males in rut fight each other, scrabbling and separating and gripping, doing pushups on the rocks betweentimes. (The pushups display their blue undersides and are thought to impress females.) Once they were under live oaks on Mount Tamalpais near the Golden Gate, once they were on the warm granite of the trail up Little Yosemite Canyon; both times I watched until all sense of scale fell away and I might as well have been watching sapphire dragons. But it is not the exceptional moments or exceptional beasts that are grounds for wonder. The everyday bluebelly found everywhere in California but the deep deserts and highest mountains is, with its purifying blood, its underside of sky, its speed and its talent for survival, already a small astonishment.

California Condor

(Gymnogyps californianus)

The condor is most dignified in flight, where it soars forever without flapping its wings, covering hundreds of miles looking for the dead things on which it feeds, its effortless travel similar to that of the smaller buzzards that are still everywhere in California. The condor, which does not build a nest but rather lays its single egg in a cave or on a ledge where it may roll to its destruction, which cools itself by excreting on its legs, whose bright red head and neck are bare so they may be stuck deep into a corpse without soaking up too much foul matter, whose young, now that the species has been reintroduced into what is no longer quite the wild, are often killed by the bottle caps and broken glass their parents feed them—the condor is not entirely enchanting. I admire wholeheartedly, however, the condor people.

In the futuristic novella *Fahrenheit 451* by Los Angeles writer Ray Bradbury, books are being burned everywhere and a secret cult of people who gather in the forest memorize a book apiece and somehow become that work of art. Books are reasonably safe for now, but animals are not, and nearly every threatened animal in California has its people, its biologists, advocates, and protectors, from the green hairstreak butterfly of San Francisco to the desert tortoise of the Mojave to the marbled murrelet of the northwest coast rainforests. Once upon a time and still in some places and cultures, people had totemic animals that protected them. These days the more fragile species have passionately dedicated people who form alliances to keep alive the animals, a little as those books were kept alive.

None have been more heroic or gone to greater lengths than the condor people, who in the 1980s located nearly every nest and bird left on earth and closely observed, hour by hour, day after day, these far-roaming creatures in rugged, remote locations, then caught them so that the species might be preserved. By 1985, there were nine free-roaming condors left on earth and a few more in zoos. The last wild condor was captured on April 20, 1987, and for some years there were none at all living free or soaring far. At the end of 2008, there were 327 of these largest North American birds, more than half living in the wild. Their fate is uncertain, for they remain vulnerable to lead pellets and bullet fragments in hunter-killed game and many other man-made perils, but without the condor people and the zoo breeding programs there would have been none at all. California is a slightly richer and stranger place now that once again thousands of miles of rough country are brushed daily by the shadows of condors with their ten-foot wingspan, while the condor people continue their work below.

California Grizzly

(Ursus arctos californicus, extinct subspecies of *Ursus arctos horribilis)*

In the old California Indian tales, women married bears and bore their children. In Mexican California, the grizzlies were lasso'd by horsemen and set to fight bulls. When the Yankees came, they raised a flag that bore a crude image of a bear and in the next sixty years or so hunted the real thing into extinction. These huge—upwards of a thousand pounds—bears were everywhere in old California; one was seen by Father Juan Crespí on what is now called Strawberry Creek in Berkeley on March 27, 1772; others are recorded in Santa Cruz, Marin County, Alameda County, Orange County, what is now Silicon Valley, the mountains of Santa Barbara and Los Angeles, herds of them on the plains of what is now urban L.A., and everywhere in the foothills

13

of the Sierra. One of the last was killed near Pasadena on May 16, 1894. The final absolutely certain sighting and killing of a wild grizzly was in 1908, though others were reported for a handful of years afterward.

It is as though the California grizzly walked out of the real world into the shadowy one called art. The bear is still visible everywhere on the state flag and on the state seal, where it stands like a loyal dog next to the incarnation of California as an armed goddess. Bears populate everyday life, from the teddy bears of children and the bear markets of Wall Street (which are said to derive their name from the way that bears swipe downward with their paws, while the bulls in the Californio bull and bear matches cut upward with their horns) to the bears, or big hairy men, who constitute a gay subculture. Animals are everywhere in our language, imaginations, dreams, and imagery, but as the animals vanish from our lives and the earth these human things become poorer, flimsier. Henry David Thoreau, who mourned the early vanishing of big animals from his northeastern corner of the country, once remarked that animals "are all beasts of burden, in a sense, made to carry some portion of our thoughts."

And what of the thoughts when the beasts of burden are gone? The appetite for them is here still, not only with children who still play with dinosaurs and teddy bears, but with adults, who go birdwatching and keep zoos and wildlife programs and countless nature programs going. We need animals who are adapted to their own needs, not ours, in a world that is bigger than us. Individual grizzlies menace individual human beings from time to time, but as a species we are menaced in shadowy but crucial ways by their absence.

California Ground Squirrel

(*Spermophilus beecheyi*)

It is perhaps a flaw of our characters that when we look at animals we see ourselves, but it is also one of the gifts of animals. A useful gift as long as we remember that it is we who are like the animals and not they who are like us. Animals allow us to reflect on our lusts and appetites, our fear of death, our desire to go on being, our attempts to solve our problems, and our anxiety when we cannot. The old bestiaries translated this into religious terms, whereby every creature was deciphered as a story of the Bible and Jesus, a guide to salvation and sin. Nowadays we are likely to see a more basic sense of the condition that is not just human but life itself, fragile, imperfect, self-renewing, occasionally incandescent, occasionally unbearable, often comic.

It is anthropocentric to say that many of the beasts of

North America have a comic appearance and disposition that is very different from European, if not from African, wildlife, but comedy, whether human or animal, is always the comedy of survival. Is there any pantheon so strange in their lineaments as the moose, the skunk, the raccoon, the opossum and the armadillo? Do any other creatures have greater power of amusing themselves than the coyote and the western raven, who are deities and creators in many native religions? The California ground squirrel is so common as to be considered a pest by farmers and gardeners, and it is a modest-looking gray-brown brindled creature whose tail is not nearly as lush as that of some of its tree-dwelling cousins, but it is a comic hero whose energetic strategies let it survive its countless predators, face off rattlesnakes as equals, and sustain a whole landscape of life.

Not always survive, for ground squirrels form a crucial part of the diet of red-tailed hawks, badgers, snakes, and other predators, so much so that the squirrels are considered to be why Sunol Regional Park, southeast of Oakland, is said to have the greatest concentration of golden eagles anywhere. But survive enough to be one of the most widespread and common mammals in the state (and despite their name their habitat stretches up to southern Washington and down to Baja). The squirrels have evolved in tandem with northern Pacific rattlesnakes, which they survive with astonishing tactics. The California ground squirrel doesn't have infrared vision, but rattlers do, which is why the squirrel has evolved a way of sending a lot of blood to its tail and then waving it around to confuse the snake about what the target is, how big it is, and how to strike it. They have a series of calls that warn each other—they live in gregarious colonies and spend most of their lives in or near their subterranean labyrinths—of predators, with different calls for different dangers. When all else fails, they attack rattlesnakes directly, and the adults have evolved what virtually no other animal has: immunity to rattlesnake venom.

So the California ground squirrel, humble, ubiquitous, annoying, prudent and defiant, is a creature whose strategies for survival are a comic success. And not for themselves alone, but for the salamanders, voles, tarantulas, and burrowing owls who take up residence in their tunnels that are an underground world unto themselves; and for the plants that benefit from the loosened soil and the seeds they turn up that then commence to grow; and for the birds, beasts and serpents they feed. They are the inglamorous, indomitable center of the grasslands ecosystem.

Chinook Salmon

(Oncorhynchus tshawytscha)

The water that evaporates off the Pacific blows in as winter storms that pile snow on the Sierra that melts and fills the streams that lead to the rivers that in the great Sacramento/San Joaquin watershed all flow to the sea, as do the smaller rain-fed streams of the Coast Ranges. Salmon follow a similar cycle, migrating inward and upward from the ocean, though they swim rather than fly, swim and thrash and leap their way upstream to their birthplace in the rivers and streams of California. In those fresh, clear waters hatch the tiny alevin that become fry and then the smolts that head downstream as they go through a drastic metamorphosis to adapt to the salt of the sea that will become their home for two or three years. They spend most of their life in this largest body of water and then, vastly increased in size, reverse the process to return to their place of birth that will also become their place of reproduction and death. For salmon, creation and death are very nearly the same act, for both males and females die soon after mating and are dying as they mate. Sometimes their flesh falls off them as they spawn. It is as though their lives were as elegant and precise as a circle: the line does not overlap itself but ends precisely where it began.

This birth that is death and the mysteries of their return to where they began are part of the charisma of salmon, as is the huge gift they represent. On this return, the mature fish bring the abundant nutrients of the open ocean back to the streams and the plants, animals, soil, and people, engendering not just the next generation of salmon but much of the landscape around them. Populations of migrating salmon are present along the whole North Pacific Rim, from Japan up through Russia, Mongolia, and Siberia across to Alaska and down the Pacific coast to central California. None of the six salmon species are endangered per se, but the runs—the evolutionarily distinct fish that return to a given river or stream—are in trouble in many places, including nearly everywhere in California. Both Central Valley spring-run and Sacramento winter-run chinook are listed as threatened or endangered by the federal government.

Salmon connect everything. When they connect the rivers to the sea and the people to the seasons, those connections are beautiful. But if you want to understand, say, the condition of a chinook on the once salmon-rich Klamath River, you need to understand the condition of the river. To understand the condition of the river you need to understand, in addition to the four dams slowing and strangling the river and making its water too sluggish and warm for the wild sea-returned fish, the condition of the land around it, and to understand the condition of the land around it you need to understand the condition of beliefs and policies about agriculture that have led to the desert being irrigated for rice on a grand scale and you also need to understand the condition of the United States economy. The fate of that salmon in the Klamath River is tied to decisions in the courts and by the corporation that owns the power-generating dams. At this time, it looks like crucial dams may come out in the biggest dam-removal project in U.S. history and the salmon may someday thrive again.

The Karuk, Yurok, and Hupa people, whose lives were once intertwined with the salmon runs, have been working to protect and bring back the fish. Salmon connect in other ways, for on the South Yuba River, upstream from the Sacramento River, the Tsi-Akim Maidu have begun to perform salmon ceremonies again after 158 years. Thanks to dams and other trouble, no salmon make it that far upriver, so the Maidu feast afterward on salmon from their allies on the Klamath. They are thus connected with the Yuba environmental community, with the Klamath tribes, with their own eroded traditions, with hopes for the future, and with the missing fish. Salmon still connect everything but that connection is uncertain now, a braided silver rope fraying, a river of gifts and dreams running low.

Desert Tortoise

(*Gopherus agassizii*)

In the Bible, Adam names all the animals. In the Oakland
Zoo, Adam is the current keeper for reptiles and insects,
and this Adam tells the story of how the zoo came to have
a desert tortoise in its care. It was entrusted by a man who
had taken the creature from the Mojave Desert when
he was twelve, long ago when no one disapproved of, let
alone outlawed, such acts. Forty-something years later, he
realized his children did not want to inherit the tortoise
and, like the larger tortoises everywhere, it was going to
live a very, very long time. We looked at the surprisingly
lively creature eating lettuce and frolicking amorously
after a much larger female tortoise of another species,
and Adam said, "The keeper who will take care of it at
the end of its days has not yet been born."

Tortoises live a long time, though desert tortoises spend so much of their time doing nothing in the cool darkness of their burrows—95 percent by one account—that it could be said they live a short, quiet life played out very, very slowly, a movie moving by at a frame a minute. And this they have been doing in the deserts of south-eastern California, southernmost Nevada and Arizona, and Mexico's coastal Sinaloa for about twelve thousand years. Often, when the males fight, the victor is the one who immobilizes his antagonist by flipping him over onto his back. They are not in a hurry, but we are, and among the threats to them are cars and off-road vehicles. Another is the raven, or rather the ravens who have proliferated in the desert, an example of how even wild animals can cease to be natural when human forces change their role, their numbers, and their interactions. The rapidly proliferating ravens are sometimes called a "subsidized species" because they live off garbage, and this easy food source makes it possible for them to colonize new territory. Desert tortoises grow as slowly as they live, and until about age five their shells are not hard enough to withstand the beaks of ravens. Picture the desert tortoise strolling calmly forward as peoples, climates, threats go by in a blur, and

pray that they will be able to stroll through the current
era into the unimaginable future and perhaps another ten
thousand years of uneventfulness.

Elephant Seal
(Mirounga angustirostris)

During their winter season, elephant seals gather on the beaches basking and flipping sand and gravel onto their backs, the males trumpeting, sparring, sometimes drawing blood, and occasionally lumbering over to mate roughly with the much smaller females, the young nursing, yelping, and dozing, a scene of sex, violence, and repose like nothing else in the world. These are the elephant seals we see, though they spend most of their lives unseen and alone in waters far from the coast. Among the few things to be grateful to the petroleum economy for is providing an alternative to whale and seal blubber late in the nineteenth century, when elephant seals and many species of whale were nearly gone. Sealers would render up to twenty-five gallons of oil from a single male, and a fat male in motion ripples and undulates as though under his thick hide he were almost as liquid as the sea. Kerosene burned as well in lamps, and petroleum was much easier to obtain than the fat of whales hunted on the open seas and seals hunted there and on the remote islands and coasts of California.

Elephant seals spend a few months a year on land, or rather on beaches, and though the species is largely aquatic, when it is on land, it is Californian. It was nearly nothing at all, being hunted into rarity by the 1850s, presumed extinct until a small herd was seen—and butchered—on the Baja, California, mainland in 1880. This was followed by the discovery and slaughter of eighty on Isla de Guadalupe in 1883, and four more were killed the following year. The species was declared extinct again until 1892, when two collectors for the Smithsonian Institution found nine on that Baja island and slaughtered seven of what they presumed were the last of their kind. Amazingly, when one of the Smithsonian collectors returned to Isla de Guadalupe in 1911, he found more than 125 on the beach. By 1922, the Mexican government had protected the elephant seal and it steadily rebounded, spreading back up the coast and through the islands around San Diego and Santa Barbara. In 1981, they began breeding north of San Francisco, in Point Reyes, their northernmost land base nowadays. There are presumed to be at least 150,000 today.

The lives of elephant seals are full of other dramatic extremes. They dive further than any other seal, reaching depths of five thousand feet—nearly a mile—and staying under for up to an hour, spend more time underwater than most whales, and are much bigger than any other seal. Their name comes not from their size but from the wobbly, fleshy hummock that is the male seal's proboscis; the males may reach five thousand pounds, while the females range from twelve hundred to two thousand pounds. Their lives are rounds of solitary feasting at sea to build up the prodigal blubber they live off during their crowded, hungry episodes on land. The females land, give birth, and go without food while transferring their stored energy as milk to their young for twenty-five to twenty-eight days, then return to sea. The abandoned pups live off their own new blubber supplies while learning to swim and dive and prepare to go to sea. The males fast during this season ashore too, because to go to sea to forage would mean losing position and control over females on the beach. And so they stay, sparring and screaming and lounging.

Mission Blue Butterfly

(Icaricia icarioides missionensis)

The day I write this, a possum in the East Bay jams the switch of the Bay Area commuter train system, stalling trains for an hour and dying in the endeavor. The great geographer Mike Davis once wrote that "metropolitan Los Angeles, now bordered primarily by mountains and desert, rather than by farmland as in the past, has the longest wild edge, abruptly juxtaposing tract houses and wildlife habitat, of any major nontropical city." The Bay Area is even more complex, a patchwork of urban and wild that melt into each other as coyotes and great blue herons take up residence in San Francisco, mountain lions roam the Oakland hills—and development moves further into what was once agricultural or wild.

Some wildlife is pressured by loss of habitat into this

urban exile, and cities menace some of the best remaining habitat. And then there are the islands in time, the places left alone as builders reshaped their surroundings, notable among them San Bruno Mountain, the muscular ridge dividing San Francisco and San Mateo Counties that is a refuge for an array of rare, unique, and endangered species. Davis described Los Angeles as an island in a sea of wild places; San Bruno Mountain rises out of an asphalt ocean as an island of wildness. The mountain is the last best habitat for three endangered butterflies, the San Bruno elfin, the Callippe checkerspot, and the mission blue. Various other species exist only there, or there and further down the Peninsula or across the Bay Area in a few other surviving spots.

But California's wildly varied terrain already formed a series of islands or patchworks long ago, marshland and grassland and forest and hilltops and serpentine soils and riparian edges and altitude changes all creating the habitats that encouraged species to evolve into local subspecies, such as the Suisun shrew in the Delta marshes, the endangered subspecies of the common ornate shrew, and the various subspecies of Boisduval's blue, a butterfly widespread across the West—of which the most famous and perhaps least common is the mission blue (unless you count the extinct Xerxes blue, whose sole habitat was the coastal lands of the

San Francisco Presidio; military expansion there during the Second World War made it one of that war's incidental casualties).

With a wingspan of little more than an inch and few who can claim to have seen it, the mission blue is already nearly invisible—but beautiful in all the drawings and photographs: the male an opalescent blue with brown edges; the female brown with a flush of blue near the base of the wings. The mission blue also occurs in the Marin Headlands, another surviving remnant of a formerly larger coastal scrub habitat. The butterfly lays its eggs on one of three species of lupine, whose leaves constitute the sole food of the caterpillar of the species, and its whole life cycle unfolds not far from these flowering bushes.

Monarch Butterfly

(Danaus plexippus)

What makes the monarch extraordinary among butterflies is often celebrated: its long migration—though
this is far more dramatic among butterflies east of the
Rockies. Those west of the mountains for the most part don't
join in the multigenerational migration to central Mexico;
they just head for the California coast, where they ride out
winter's cold clustered into eucalyptus and pine trees. What
makes all butterflies, including monarchs, remarkable, are
the four dramatically different phases of their life cycle.
Something of that astonishment—the extremity of the
transformations—is present in the names given to the three
stages of a butterfly's life after the egg hatches. In Latin and
scientific language, the caterpillar is a larva, which also means
ghost or mask, and the chrysalis is a pupa, or doll, from which

we also get the word puppet. The Greek word for the adult butterfly is also their word for soul: psyche. A ghost becomes a doll; the doll becomes a soul. Crawling becomes stillness becomes flight.

Monarchs are tied to the milkweed plant, the sole food of the larva and the source of the bitterness that makes the butterfly unpalatable to birds and other potential predators. It is on milkweed that the female deposits her eggs, one at a time, each on the underside of its own leaf, after the long, long copulatory rite that is also typical of many butterflies, lasting many hours or even overnight (an amazing duration for a creature whose life is measured in weeks or months). The prolonged lovemaking may be a strategy to decrease the chances the female will mate with other males, and some monarch studies suggest that sperm is not even transferred until after nightfall.

The eggs of monarchs are said to be unusually beautiful: translucent fluted beads. The larva becomes increasingly garishly striped in white, yellow, and black as it increases in weight about three thousand times; it grows from a few millimeters to several centimeters through its five instars, or phases of development, between each of which it splits its skin and a newer, larger caterpillar emerges. The pupa lurks within the last of the five instars, so that the many-legged creature splits out of its skin one last time to become a legless, motionless, inert being—and a beautiful one: in its early stages, the monarch's chrysalis is celadon green with a gold line and gold dots, dangling like a strange ornament from whatever twig or leaf it has bound itself to. And then comes the monarch we all know, the one with broad black lines along the veins of its wings, like the leading in stained glass, deep orange panels and white spots on a black border. Or think we know, but we hardly know our own souls either.

Mountain Lion
(*Puma concolor* or *Felis concolor*)

I have never actually seen a mountain lion in the wild, though once a man I was looking back at near Pinnacles National Monument suddenly looked surprised: a mountain lion had strolled across the hillside behind me but was gone before I turned. I knew a few people who saw the mountain lions who returned to the Marin Headlands at the end of the 1980s—and it was and is extraordinary to think of lions that can see San Francisco; perhaps a lion is why a deer once ran across the Golden Gate Bridge. I know the ranger who recovered the body of the woman jogger who was killed by a female lion in the Sierra in 1994, and I housed friends who came up to visit the hospitalized man who had survived an attack in Humboldt County in 2007 because his wife beat the animal into retreat. Mountain lions are seemingly everywhere, including suburban Silicon Valley, the Oakland Hills, and Los Angeles's wild edges, but that doesn't mean most of us will ever see them. Even so, their presence changes everything. They are a constant reminder that we are not truly entirely atop the food chain; in the eyes of one animal a lot of us register as game about the size of a deer. They make the landscape back into what it once was, a place that requires intense and continual awareness of surroundings and possibilities, a place that wakes you up, as distinct from the confidently drowsy inattention possible in truly domesticated landscapes.

The mountain lion has officially been eliminated from the eastern half of the United States except for a tiny relict population in Florida, but one does occasionally show up, and unconfirmed sightings of the "cat of god" and "ghost cat" still occur in the East. In the West, they have joined a number of other species—ravens and coyotes in particular—who are moving into the edges of the human environment, in part because that's what's left, in part because most of us are not hunters anymore. The century and a half in which mountain lions disappeared from the East, tule elk from the marshes, whales from the sea, and all kinds of birds and fishes from all kinds of rivers and skies were about hunting and habitat loss. The new era that began perhaps half a century ago continues depredation by poisons and habitat loss but also has let up on hunting, restricted some poisons and pollutions, and given rise to the kinds of animal people who have done so much for so many species—and there is a Mountain Lion Foundation in California. Climate change may trump all that in terms of species loss, but for now we are in an odd game with the animals. In forcing them into new overlaps with the human, we are creating situations in which urban and rural, wild and civilized no longer divide the world so neatly. Mountain lions are perhaps the best emblem of that change. But they are not merely emblems; they are something to think about whenever you go into the landscape.

Tule Elk

(Cervus elaphus nannodes)

A Russian traveler up the coast north of San Francisco wrote in 1824 of seeing elk "as large as a horse, with branching antlers; these generally graze on hills, from whence they can see round them on all sides, and appear much more cautious than the small ones"—more cautious than the deer, that is. From a distance a tule elk might be mistaken for a deer, and they are the smallest of the American elk, but at closer range the differences are clear. Tule elk, with their dark necks curving like a ship's prow up from the solid caramel-tan block of their faceted bodies and their white rumps that are also faceted, look as though they were carved from pine, walnut, and oak. They move in herds, often, and though most have not been hunted in generations they retain their alertness to any sound or smell and, alarmed, will move

45

away swiftly, the loose scatter of grazing beasts tightening into a knot that flows over the land like the shadow of a wind-driven cloud.

Once, tule elk were almost everywhere in coastal California, an estimated half-million of them in the Coast Ranges and the Central Valley when that valley was almost as rich as an African savannah, with elk, deer, pronghorns, bison, feral horses, grizzlies, coyotes, wolves all roaming freely. The first few decades after the Gold Rush saw them hunted into near nonexistence. They were thought to be extinct, earlier than the grizzly, simultaneous with the elephant seal, until workers for cattle baron Henry Miller found a few hiding in the tule reeds of Miller's vast San Joaquin Valley holdings. Though in other ways he was destroying the wild California landscape, Miller himself did much to keep the few alive and let them multiply, and then the state of California took over, and the species is secure. Now they exist in a handful of refuges, about four thousand of them from the Eastern Sierra high desert to the tip of Tomales Peninsula north of San Francisco, Grizzly Island in the Delta, and the hills southeast of the Bay Area. There they graze, fight, mate, give birth, and die, hunted a little by humans, mountain lions, and coyotes but secure to continue in the uncertain landscape of California, the only place they occur.

There are plenty of species that remain relatively stable

and likely to survive without intervention, from bluebellies to California quail, jackrabbits to sea lions. And many that are thriving and moving into the human-made landscape, including coyotes, raccoons, ravens, and crows. Perhaps the human population will shrink radically, seasonal waters will reclaim the great Central Valley, and tule elk will recover their habitat, or some other expansion will take place; they are ready, and the several herds around the state are flourishing. Perhaps not. They barely survived one moment of our history, we chose to protect them in another moment, and what comes next for them is unknown. The future of California and the earth is unfathomable at present, for human beings as well as for the thousands of other species here. It depends on choices we make now, and surprises we cannot anticipate.

About the Author

The author of this book, Rebecca Solnit, grew up near the north end of the San Francisco Bay, where she crossed paths with a great many bluebelly lizards, as well as ringneck, garter, and gopher snakes, mule deer, quail, raccoons, buzzards, tadpoles, dragonflies, and other Californians. With a few interruptions she has lived in the Bay Area ever since, though she has spent a lot of time in the Great Basin and Mojave deserts and some in the Sierra. Among her dozen books many have California, San Francisco, and western landscapes and nature as their subject. These include *Secret Exhibition; Savage Dreams; Wanderlust: A History of Walking; A Field Guide to Getting Lost;* and *River of Shadows.*

About the Artist

The grandfather of this book's artist, Mona Caron, was a botanical illustrator in Switzerland. She herself grew up in the Swiss Italian Alps, among rivers, mosses, ferns, goats, and lizards. It is an area particularly rich in lizards, including the sapphire-bellied Smaragdeidechsen, or emerald lizard. As a child she dissected flowers on her own time, when she was supposed to be listening to lessons, and as an adult she moved to San Francisco and studied illustration and subsequently became one of the city's premiere muralists. Much of her work deals with human history and utopian possibility, and most of it depicts natural history, from her butterfly-themed Brisbane mural to the wildflower-studded Duboce Bikeway mural and the colossal vegetables of the Noe Valley Farmer's Market mural, or the Market Street Railway mural in San Francisco.

About the Project

A *California Bestiary* was born when the founding director of Heyday Books, Malcolm Margolin, proposed a collaboration with the Oakland Zoo, which is developing an ambitious educational exhibit, called "*California!*," that will celebrate native California flora and fauna by focusing on conservation and cultural importance. When Rebecca Solnit was invited to be the writer, she brought along her friend Mona Caron to begin a collaboration between images and words and between artists and the Oakland Zoo. At the zoo, the two pondered the nature of the human fascination with other species. They visited with keepers, saw elephants being lovingly tended, were chased—slowly—by tortoises, witnessed a hedgehog dental extraction, and had other adventures that illuminated the job of caring for animals and educating people at this zoo that has set new standards in animal welfare.

The animals in this book were chosen to reflect the enormous diversity of California's many ecological zones; the broad range of survival status, from severely threatened to thriving; and the pure, glorious presence of so many kinds of extraordinary other Californians—though picking only twelve meant leaving out pipevine swallowtails, Steller's jays, kangaroo rats, coyotes, red-tailed hawks, snowy plovers, and other creatures dear to the authors' hearts. The medieval bestiaries were books about animals seen through a window of wonder, and *A California Bestiary* is a twenty-first-century endeavor to work in this vein.

Mona and Rebecca would like to thank Nik Haas-Dehejia at the Oakland Zoo and Jeff Kinzley, the elephant curator there; Derek Hitchcock of the Source to Sea Project for conversations about salmon; Deirdre Elmansoumi for friendship and butterfly wisdom; Jack Laws for general animal consulting; and the staffs of the San Francisco Public Library and the Life Sciences Library at the University of California, Berkeley. Mona would also like to thank Nicholas Kasimatis for precious feedback and support.

Malcolm Margolin and the staff of Heyday would like to thank Rebecca and Mona for their intellectual and artistic generosity; Dr. Joel Parrott, executive director of the Oakland Zoo, for opening the gates so welcomingly; and the Creative Work Fund for allowing us this opportunity.

HEYDAY INSTITUTE

Since its founding in 1974, Heyday Books has occupied a unique niche in the publishing world, specializing in books that foster an understanding of the history, literature, art, environment, social issues, and culture of California and the West. We are a 501(c)(3) nonprofit organization based in Berkeley, California, serving a wide range of people and audiences.

We are grateful for the generous funding we've received for our publications and programs during the past year from foundations and more than three hundred and fifty individual donors. Major supporters include:

Anonymous; Audubon California; Judith and Phillip Auth; Barona Band of Mission Indians; B.C.W. Trust III; S. D. Bechtel, Jr. Foundation; Barbara and Fred Berensmeier; Berkeley Civic Arts Program and Civic Arts Commission; Joan Berman; Peter and Mimi Buckley; Lewis and Sheana Butler; Butler Koshland Fund; California State Automobile Association; California State Coastal Conservancy; California State Library; Joanne Campbell; Candelaria Fund; John and Nancy Cassidy Family Foundation, through Silicon Valley Community Foundation; Creative Work Fund; Columbia Foundation; The Community Action Fund; Community Futures Collective; Compton Foundation, Inc.; Lawrence Crooks; Eaton Kenyon Fund of the Sacramento Region Community Foundation; Ida Rae Egli; Donald and Janice Elliott, in honor of David Elliott, through Silicon Valley Community Foundation; Evergreen

Foundation; Federated Indians of Graton Rancheria; Mark and Tracy Ferron; Furthur Foundation; George Gamble; Wallace Alexander Gerbode Foundation; Richard & Rhoda Goldman Fund; Ben Graber, in honor of Sandy Graber; Evelyn & Walter Haas, Jr. Fund; Walter & Elise Haas Fund; James and Coke Hallowell; Cheryl Hinton; James Irvine Foundation; Marty and Pamela Krasney; Robert and Karen Kustel, in honor of Bruce Kelley; Guy Lampard and Suzanne Badenhoop; LEF Foundation; Michael McCone; National Endowment for the Arts; National Park Service; Organize Training Center; Patagonia; Pease Family Fund, in honor of Bruce Kelley; Resources Legacy Fund; Alan Rosenus; San Francisco Foundation; San Manuel Band of Mission Indians; Deborah Sanchez; Contee and Maggie Seely; James B. Swinerton; Swinerton Family Fund; Taproot Foundation; Thendara Foundation; Lisa Van Cleef and Mark Gunson; Marion Weber; Albert and Susan Wells; Dean Witter Foundation; and Yocha Dehe Wintun Nation.

For more information about Heyday Institute, our publications and programs, please visit our website at www.heydaybooks.com.